Eltham Palace

Michael Turner, MVO

Introduction

Eltham Palace was once an important royal palace, playing host to kings and queens and international statesmen. It is one of the few medieval royal palaces in England to survive with substantial remains intact and was one of only six palaces large enough to accommodate and feed the entire Tudor court. Initially a moated manor house, it was acquired by the future Edward II (r.1307–27) in 1305. Under Edward IV (r.1461–83) significant changes were made, most notably the addition in the 1470s of the great hall, which still stands today. Eltham Palace was eclipsed by Greenwich and Hampton Court palaces in the 16th century and declined in the early 17th century. For 200 years after the Civil Wars it was used as a farm.

In the 1930s Stephen and Virginia Courtauld were looking for a semi-rural property within easy reach of central London. Eltham met their requirements and the architects Seely and Paget built a house for them adjoining the great hall, boasting an ultra-modern design and using the latest technology. Leading designers and craftsmen were employed to create a range of lavish interiors and outstanding gardens, providing the setting for their extensive collection of art and furniture, and ample space for entertaining.

The Courtaulds left Eltham in 1944 and the site was occupied by Army educational units until 1992. English Heritage assumed management of the entire site in 1995, and in 1999 completed a major programme of repairs and restoration of the 1930s house and gardens.

This guidebook contains a description of the remarkable 1930s interiors, the medieval remains and the gardens, followed by an account of the development and history of this extraordinary site.

Facing page: A winter view of Eltham Palace's copper-clad loggia seen from the garden to the east

Below: Portrait bust of Virginia Courtauld commissioned from Count Filippo Lovatelli in Rome, 1923

Tour of the House

The tour starts with the exterior of the 1930s building. Inside, it takes in the Swedish-designed entrance hall, refurnished Italian drawing room and private ground-floor rooms of Stephen and Ginie Courtauld, before reaching the 15th-century great hall of the former royal palace – a striking contrast to the 1930s interiors. Small displays relating to the Courtaulds and the Army are exhibited on the first floor, where there is a good view of the great hall from the minstrels' gallery. The tour continues to the family and guest bedroom suites and the sleeping quarters of Ginie's pet lemur. Returning to the ground floor, the tour culminates in the fully restored Art Deco dining room.

FOLLOWING THE TOUR
The numbers beside the headings highlight the key points on the tour and correspond with the small numbered plans in the margins.

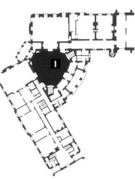

Left: The turning circle and main entrance to Eltham Palace. Elaborate lead rainwater heads incorporate Stephen and Ginie's initials, coats of arms and the date 1935 in Roman numerals

Below left: Vesta, the Roman goddess of hearth, home and family, by Harry Carlton Attwood

Facing page: Entrance hall marquetry panel by Jerk Werkmäster, showing the Palazzo Vecchio, Florence (left), and the church of Santa Maria della Salute, Venice (right)

EXTERIOR

Visitors enter the house built by the Courtaulds in the 1930s. The curved entrance colonnade is flanked by two tall, copper-clad pavilions with models of chessmen on the roof ridges. The green-painted steel casement windows by Henry Hope and Son are typical of the 1930s. The infilled arches of the colonnade are inspired by Sir Christopher Wren's Hampton Court and the library at Trinity College, Cambridge (attended by the architects Seely and Paget). The junction between the 1930s building and the medieval great hall to the right is marked by a projecting spiral staircase with a stone cap. Sculpture decorates the outside of the 1930s house: over the arch to the main entrance is a work by H Carlton Attwood depicting the goddess Vesta, inviting you to enter.

▮ ENTRANCE HALL

To the left and right are the gentlemen's and ladies' cloakrooms – an arrangement more typical of an institution than a private house, but reflecting the importance of entertaining at Eltham.

Glazed double doors lead into the entrance hall, which is triangular in plan with curved sides. Light floods in through the concrete glass domed roof, which is 7m in diameter – a feature requested by Stephen Courtauld. The interior design of this space was by the Swedish architect and designer Rolf Engströmer (1892–1970), whose work Stephen and Virginia may have seen on a trip to Stockholm in 1928.

The hall is lined with Australian blackbean veneer, incorporating marquetry panels by the Swedish artist Jerk Werkmäster (1896–1978) on either side of the entrance doors. The panels represent the southern and northern limits of European civilization: a Roman soldier and a Viking against background scenes from Italy and Scandinavia. Some of the Courtaulds' favourite buildings are represented, including palaces in Florence and Venice and buildings in Stockholm such as the 1920s town hall by Ragnar Ostberg. Engströmer's refined design was described in 1937 in *Country Life* as 'probably the first example in this country of modern Swedish decoration originated

Right: The entrance hall. The marquetry panels by Werkmäster show Italian buildings and a Roman centurion guarding the room
Below: Scenes from Lewis Carroll's Alice's Adventures in Wonderland by the surrealist sculptor Eric Grate

by Ostberg at the Stockholm Town Hall', which was a place of pilgrimage for young British architects at the time. Above the entrance are two plaques created by another Swede, Eric Grate (1896–1983), depicting scenes from Lewis Carroll's *Alice* books.

A circular rug by the well-established and influential textile and carpet designer Marion Dorn, measuring 5.8m in diameter, was commissioned for the centre of the hall. Its shades of reddish brown, pinkish beige and fawn complemented the marquetry designs on the walls, and the pattern was intended to draw visitors into the drawing and dining rooms. (The present rug is a replica of the original, which is now at the Victoria and Albert Museum.) The replica entrance hall curtains have horizontal bands; the originals were doubtless also designed by Dorn. The blackbean and walnut furniture – including a cocktail cabinet holding pre-dinner drinks, and chairs with fashionable cream loose covers edged with piping – was designed by Engströmer for this room; on display are replicas based on the original designs in the Swedish Museum of Architecture, Stockholm.

At the far side of the entrance hall, to the left of the French windows, is a booth containing a coin-operated telephone for the use of guests making outside calls.

Above: A 1930s coin-operated telephone. A telephone like this would have been used by guests to make outside calls
Below: Stockholm buildings depicted in the entrance hall marquetry panels by Werkmaster include the dome of Gustav Vasa church, Ostberg's town hall (centre) and the tower of St Nicholas's Church and the royal palace (behind and to the right)

Above: Mah-Jongg's bamboo ladder leading from the flower room to his sleeping quarters
Right: The recreated flower room, which was used for preparing and arranging cut flowers
Below right: Peter Malacrida and his wife Nadja, who were good friends of the Courtaulds. Malacrida designed some of the interiors at Eltham

2 FLOWER ROOM

Opposite the telephone booth is the flower room, which retains one of the few surviving 1930s metal windows. The room was used for preparing and arranging cut flowers supplied by the gardener, which were an important feature of the house. About 90 glass, porcelain and pottery flower vases and bowls were stored here in the 1930s. The original sink and cupboards were removed by the Army and the current fittings have been recreated using Seely and Paget's original design drawing. A bamboo ladder next to the entrance leads to a trapdoor which enabled Ginie's pet ring-tailed lemur, Mah-Jongg, to come down from his first-floor quarters during the daytime.

3 DRAWING ROOM

The drawing room was sumptuously decorated. A hint of the original appearance of this room is provided by the reproduction soft furnishings: silk-damask curtains and sofas covered in blue velvet. The room was designed by the interior designer and socialite Peter Malacrida for the firm White Allom. It incorporates a number of items salvaged from the music room of the Courtaulds' former home in London at 47 Grosvenor Square, which Malacrida may have installed there in the 1920s. These include the cupboard doors on either side of the entrance doors and the dark green iron screens to the French windows beside the chimneybreast. The marble fireplace is Italian in inspiration and was probably designed by Malacrida, while the painted decoration on the false plaster beams imitates Hungarian folk art (the combination referring to Ginie's Italo-Hungarian parentage). The hollow beams accommodated concealed lighting directed on to the paintings – a sophisticated device then recently imported from Paris. The walls and ceilings were painted cream, with an added refinement of a thin honey-coloured glaze on top.

The plaster panels in the window reveals were designed by Gilbert Ledward (1888–1960) in 1935. They refer to the ideas of the German philosopher

Peter Malacrida (1889–1980)

Peter Malacrida (the Marchese Malacrida de Saint-August) was an eccentric Italian aristocrat, who wore two pairs of socks and had something of a reputation as a playboy. Just after the First World War he became a newspaper correspondent and in 1922 married Nadja Green, who wrote plays under the pen name Lewis Hope. The Malacridas were personal friends of the Courtauld family. They were great entertainers and popular with the 'young West End set', according to the author Cecil Roberts. Malacrida took to interior design, specializing in a Florentine Renaissance style. In the late 1920s and early 1930s he and his wife were near neighbours of Stephen and Ginie in Grosvenor Square, and he carried out work for them and for Sam Courtauld, Stephen's brother. His designs were regarded as sensational, although one contemporary dismissed him as a 'phoney'.

During the 1930s depression, Malacrida joined the firm White Allom, where his social contacts with clients were extremely useful. In 1940, however, he returned to Italy to fight for Mussolini in the war. He subsequently retired to Ireland.

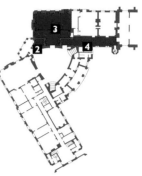

Left: *The drawing room photographed in 1936. Above the chimneypiece is the large 16th-century painting* The Contest of Apollo and Marsyas *by Jacopo Tintoretto (originally intended for a ceiling) and to the left is Cosimo Rosselli's 15th-century Madonna, clothed in rich dark blue and red robes*

Oswald Spengler expounded in *The Decline of the West* (first published in English in 1926). Paired panels represent the four quarters of the world (northern, southern, eastern and western) illustrating various contrasting civilizations throughout history. The first pair depicts northern civilization; intellectuals equated Caesarism with Nazism, whose rise they viewed with alarm. The decline of civilization through decadence would result in mankind once again being forced to live off the land as an eternal peasant. Spengler's theory of decline appealed to Ledward in relation to modern art, particularly the move away from realism towards abstraction. Presumably Stephen Courtauld was also sympathetic to these views. Above each relief are alternate coats of arms of the Courtaulds and the Peiranos (the latter representing a lion grasping a pear tree).

The floor was laid with antique 'Turkish' rugs. The room was designed to display the Courtaulds' collection of Italian walnut furniture, antiques and works of art including two paintings by the Italian Renaissance painter Paolo Veronese – *Astronomer* and *Patriarch,* on the wall opposite the chimneypiece (on loan from the National Gallery of Zimbabwe) – and the most outstanding single painting in the collection, *Descent into Limbo* (see page 47) by the Renaissance painter Andrea Mantegna (now in a private collection). Where necessary, alternative paintings have been hung to give an impression of the original effect.

The cupboards and niches housed Stephen's important collection of almost 30 pieces of Italian ceramics – mostly 16th-century Maiolica, whose vibrant colours would have acted as a foil to the cream-coloured walls.

4 GREAT HALL CORRIDOR

All the floors were cleaned by a vacuum hose fixed to skirting sockets, which were linked to the basement vacuum cleaner. Above the door to the great hall corridor is a loudspeaker which was connected to a mahogany record cabinet in the corridor, from which music could be broadcast to some of the ground-floor rooms. Next to it was a wireless set with seven pairs of speakers in a cabinet designed to look like an old Italian walnut cassone (coffer).

5 BOUDOIR

Ginie Courtauld's sycamore-panelled boudoir was designed by Peter Malacrida. During the war, when the drawing room was closed up, the boudoir became the central focus of the house, presided over by Ginie and also Congo, her parrot, whose cage was here. The fashion for ceilings to be painted a lighter tint of the wall colour can be seen here, as in many of the main rooms. The ribbed, coved and mirrored ceiling with its concealed lighting is Art Deco-inspired. The sofa, framed by shelves, is an early example of built-in furniture. It has Italian *trapunto* quilted cushions with a raised design (quilting was a popular hobby in the 1930s). The room housed nearly 600 books, 95 of which were French novels, and also a walnut McMichael wireless set with an art silk cover (McMichael radios were hand-made and considered to be the best available). Above the sofa is a large painting by Jan Wyck, *Frost Fair on the Thames in 1684*.

An arch to the right of the sofa led to the secretary's office. It contained three telephones – part of the internal and external system. In 1939 this room was described as the map room because maps were pasted to the walls to help the Courtaulds' secretary to arrange their overseas tours. Some of the maps survive beneath the modern wallpaper and it is hoped that this room can be restored at a later date.

Leather map

In the later 17th and early 18th centuries it was fashionable for property-owners to display maps and bird's-eye views of their estates. The leather map above the fireplace, depicting Eltham Palace and its surroundings, is a revival of this tradition. It combines a map with topographical views and was created in Paris by Margarita Classen-Smith, an accomplished worker of appliqué-leather. It incorporates a jib (hidden) door (now not in use) linking Ginie's boudoir with Stephen's library.

John Seely and Paul Paget

Henry John Alexander Seely (1899–1963) was the eldest surviving son of the 1st Baron Mottistone. He read architecture at Trinity College, Cambridge, where he met Paul Edward Paget (1901–85). Seely and Paget established their firm in April 1926, with Paget running the administrative side of the office and fostering contacts with potential clients. They installed themselves at Queen's Square Mews in London, where other residents included the architects Edwin Lutyens and Aston Webb, and Edward Hudson, founder of *Country Life*, a magazine which reported some of Seely and Paget's early work enthusiastically. Their first domestic job was the restoration and alteration of Mottistone Manor on the Isle of Wight for Seely's father; minor domestic alterations for the actress Gladys Cooper and the playwright J B Priestley followed. By 1931 the firm had moved to 41 Cloth Fair, where it remained until 1986.

Other early work included church

commissions such as St Faith, Lee-on-Solent, Hampshire (built between 1933 and 1934), but Eltham Palace was Seely and Paget's most important and ambitious project to date. They built up a close relationship with their clients, picnicking with the Courtaulds in the grounds during construction of the new house and staying with them afterwards on several occasions. The Second World War later created opportunities for both secular and church restoration jobs, including repairs to a significant number of bomb-damaged London churches.

Right: Paul Paget and John Seely in 1935 discussing Eltham Palace in the Shack on the Isle of Wight – the cliff-top holiday home/office they designed at Mottistone Manor

Above: A 1930s magazine advertisement for a McMichael radio, similar to the one at Eltham

Left: The boudoir and built-in sofa. Country Life commented in 1932: 'One of the most sensible and convenient of recent pieces of furniture is the couch that combines shelves for the current library books and crossword dictionaries, with place to put down a cup of tea or a glass'

Leather map of Eltham and its surroundings

A Eltham Palace

B The Woolwich coat of arms. Below is the Crystal Palace at Sydenham, which burned down in November 1936

C The Thames by the former Royal Naval College and domed Observatory

D A synchronous electric clock built into the map

E The jib door showing Napoleon III and his consort Eugénie, who lived in exile at Chislehurst in 1871

Right: The library, which served as Stephen's study
Below: Modern copy of Charles Sargeant Jagger's The Sentry, 1922, the reduced version of his war memorial at Watts Warehouse (now the Britannia Hotel), Manchester
Below right: Watercolour of Brunnen, Lake Lucerne by J M W Turner, c.1843, now in the Courtauld Institute, but originally on display in the library at Eltham

6 LIBRARY

The library, also by Malacrida, is lined with what *Country Life* described as 'Indian mahogany'. It accommodated Stephen's collection of watercolours and other topographical works by 18th- and 19th-century artists such as J R Cozens, Paul Sandby, Thomas Girtin and John Sell Cotman. They included 13 Turners, which are now in the Courtauld Institute (those on display are copies). They were protected by ingenious vertically sliding shutters designed by Stephen, probably inspired by a similar arrangement in Sir John Soane's house in Lincoln's Inn Fields. On the outside of the shutters was a collection of woodcuts, etchings and engravings, including works by the German Renaissance artist Albrecht Dürer and Turner.

Among the books were standard reference works such as the *Dictionary of National Biography* and the *Encyclopaedia Britannica*, as well as those representing more specialist interests such as mountaineering, exploration, Greek and Roman coins, history, art and gardening. Architectural and topographical books included works on the medieval palace of Eltham, which Stephen used to write a guidebook to the palace. The library also housed Stephen's extensive collection of English lustreware porcelain and his coin collection.

The walnut desk (a replica) sits in front of a recess housing a pull-down roller map. Stephen's telephone is hidden in an adjacent cupboard. Opposite is a fireplace, with a niche above containing a bronze statuette, *The Sentry*. This sculpture was purchased from Charles Sargeant Jagger in 1924 as a reduced copy of his war memorial in Manchester. Like Stephen, Jagger had joined the Artists' Rifles during the First World War and was awarded the Military Cross in 1918. The profound significance of the subject for Stephen Courtauld is suggested by its prominent position in the room. The present statuette is a cast of the original.

Left: Stephen and Ginie entertaining in Scotland in about 1946. The guests include August Courtauld (sitting second from the left, in front of Stephen), his daughter Perina (centre), Mollie Courtauld (standing behind Ginie) and Rear-Admiral L Stanley Holbrook and his wife Gladys

Stephen and Virginia Courtauld

Stephen Courtauld (1883–1967) was the youngest of six children. The family owned a highly successful business empire manufacturing rayon (then known as artificial or art silk). Stephen did not join the firm, but his inherited shares generated a substantial fortune, which he used to pursue a variety of cultural and philanthropic interests. At the onset of the First World War Stephen joined the Artists' Rifles. In 1918 he was awarded the Military Cross and rose to the rank of major in the Machine Gun Corps. After the war he resumed one of his greatest passions – mountaineering in the Alps. In 1919 he completed the pioneer ascent of the Innominata face of Mont Blanc with E G Oliver.

Stephen met Virginia Peirano at Courmayeur in the Alps. 'Ginie' was born in Romania in about 1881, the daughter of an Italian father and Hungarian mother, and was a marchesa (marchioness) by her unhappy first marriage to an Italian aristocrat, Paul Spinola. Stephen and Ginie were married in August 1923 by the British Consul in Fiume. It was an attraction of opposites. Ginie had a lively Italian temperament: vivacious, full of laughter, unconventional, impulsive and chic – she had a

snake tattooed just above her right ankle reputedly as a dare when a teenager. Stephen, on the other hand, was intensely intellectual, and had been affected by his experiences in the war. He was cautious and reserved; he thought much, but said little. A former colleague wrote: 'he was very much our Rock of Gibraltar – always the same, good days and bad, completely unflappable. He never used two words where one would do.'

They had no children, but from 1926 they looked after Ginie's two nephews – Peter (1916–2006) and Paul Peirano (1918–42). The couple also enthusiastically supported the arts. Stephen was a trustee of Covent Garden Opera House and he made a large donation towards building the Courtauld Galleries in the Fitzwilliam Museum, Cambridge. In 1926 he built the London Ice Club, the first post-war ice-skating rink in the country, in John Islip Street, Westminster. Ginie hosted charity events there, attended by celebrities of the day. In 1933 she redecorated it in a colour scheme comprising 'the shade of the inside leaves of a lettuce' and 'peach with a touch of sunburn in it'. War forced the Ice Club to close in 1940.

Stephen 'was very much our Rock of Gibraltar ... He never used two words where one would do'

7

Right: The great hall corridor. Malacrida intended the walls to be decorated and lined to imitate stone blocks using Stic B – a matt paint originally formulated for covering rough cement, but which became popular for decorative schemes in the 1930s
Below: Detail from the Chinese incised lacquer screen leading to the great hall

Facing page: The great hall from the south bay window – a fusion of restored 15th-century hammerbeam roof and stonework, 1936 stained glass depicting Bishop Odo, timber roof ornaments and modern reproductions of Seely's gondola-style lanterns

7 GREAT HALL

At the end of the corridor leading to the great hall is a 12-panelled Chinese lacquer Coromandel screen (so-called because they were exported to Europe in large quantities via the Coromandel coast of south-east India). Beyond the screen is the great hall. Although this was incorporated into the 1930s house, the hall was originally part of the medieval palace, and was built for Edward IV in the 1470s.

Like most medieval great halls, it is composed of a high end, with a raised platform or dais where the king or lord would once have dined, and a low, or service, end with a screens passage, which shielded the main hall from draughts from the external doors. The two blocked openings in the passage led to the buttery and pantry. The kitchens were in a courtyard beyond the door at the far end of the passage. In front of the blocked openings is a display of archaeological remains excavated on site, an acknowledgement to Stephen's own small display of prints and archaeological finds.

The craftsmen responsible for the hall were presumably the king's master-mason, Thomas Jordan, and the king's master-carpenter, Edmund Graveley. The hall was one of the largest in medieval England and is comparable in size with the great hall at Hampton Court, built in the 1530s. It measures 30.8m by 10.9m and is 16.8m high to the apex of the roof. The magnificent oak roof is

an elaborate hammerbeam construction with the short vertical posts morticed into the ends of the archbraced horizontal hammerbeams. This is one of the first buildings to combine hammerbeams with pendants. Curved wind braces give strength to the roof trusses. The fine tracery was once partly gilded. Near the dais end of the hall was a hearth, with a hexagonal louvre in the roof above for smoke to escape (the current framing for the louvre dates from the 1930s). The rest of the floor was originally tiled. The high windows allowed light to flood in and were decorated with stained glass. The extensive wall space below was probably initially blank to accommodate expensive tapestries when the court was in residence, although by 1649 the hall is described as 'garnished with wainescote' (panelling).

At the dais end two double-height rectangular bay windows give further light and emphasis to the most important part of the hall. Some of the damaged stone ornaments to the vaulting in each bay were replaced in timber by Seely and Paget. Two doors in the end bays originally led to the king's and queen's apartments beyond the hall, and the blind windows above them probably once lit the stairs and landings beyond. The doorways now lead to the orangery and squash court, added by the Courtaulds.

The Courtaulds intended the great hall to be used as a music room. They carried out repairs to the medieval walls, introduced modern comforts such as central-heating pipes under the floor and made a series of interventions that might be described as 'antiquarian revival'. These changes represent Stephen Courtauld's (and his architects') view of what a medieval great hall should be like. They may also have been influenced by the contemporary film industry's view of Tudor England: in 1933, the year the Courtaulds found Eltham, Charles Laughton starred in the acclaimed film *The Private Life of Henry VIII*. The minstrels' gallery and its balustrade were created by the Courtaulds. The timber screen at the dais end – also a speculative addition by Seely and Paget – was based on the 15th-century rood screen in Attleborough Church, Norfolk. Above the canopy are coloured shields of various monarchs associated with the hall from Edward II to Henry VIII, while beneath are the date 1935 and the initials of individuals responsible for the restoration, including

Right: A visiting RAF
serviceman and the Great
Dane Caesar photographed
in the great hall in 1940 by
Iliffe Cozens, Commanding
Officer RAF Hemswell
Below: Mah-Jongg, carved by
Graham and Groves on one
of the timber bosses to the
vaulting in the north bay of
the great hall

JWH (John Hopkins, clerk of works), SLC and VC (Stephen and Ginie), CP (Charles Peers), JS (John Seely), PEP (Paul Paget) and WMK (the painter Winifred [Monnington] Knights).

Stained glass was added in 1936 by George Kruger Gray, a master of heraldic design and one of the foremost designers of coins, medals and stained glass. The roundels depict the badges of Edward IV: the sun in splendour, the Yorkist white rose, the two combined as the 'rose en soleil' and the falcon and fetterlock. Stained glass in the bay windows at the dais end depicts bishops Odo and Bek and the coats of arms of Edward I, Edward III, Richard II and Henry VIII in the south bay and Edward IV and his queen Elizabeth in the north. On the walls are modern copies of the ten metal

sconces with coronet surmounts, which were probably designed by Seely; behind these hung art silk hangings made by Courtaulds and given by Stephen's brother Sam. The current hangings date from the 1960s.

The restoration was commemorated by a Latin inscription in the southern bay window carved by Percy Smith; it can be translated as: 'This hall, which the great King Edward built in former days, having fallen into increasing ruin, has now been restored through the care of Virginia and Stephen.' Below, in English, is an inscription summarizing the history of the site, which was added at the suggestion of Queen Mary: 'This hall was built by Edward IV in the year 1479, the bridge over the moat by Richard II in 1396 and the moat walls by Antony Bek, bishop of Durham about the year 1300.'

The Courtaulds filled their 1930s version of a medieval hall with antique furniture – mostly 17th-century English and European – which remains in the hall today. Much of this was purchased specifically for the great hall, including the large 'Welsh yew' table intended for the centre of the hall and the 16th-century oak refectory table, which is 6.4m long. Although 1930s and 1940s photographs show the room in use as a sitting room, the great hall really came into its own as a reception room for large parties.

The adjoining dressing room contains a further display about the Army's occupation of Eltham. The room could be used as a single bedroom if necessary with its own *en suite* bathroom. The bathrooms have chrome fittings and often a sunken bath with a shelf alongside. This particular bathroom retains nearly all its original fittings.

⑩ MINSTRELS' GALLERY

Seely and Paget created a minstrels' gallery by making an opening through the east wall of the great hall, flooring over the screens passage and adding a balustrade. This provided a superb view of the great hall. Music recitals were sometimes given here; in 1939 the gallery housed a Bechstein upright grand piano. A smaller door leads to the spiral staircase connecting the roof parapet and the basement billiard room. Scorch marks on the floor and balcony were caused by an incendiary bomb which damaged the roof during the battle of Britain in September 1940.

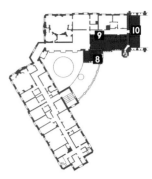

Left: The west staircase in 1936. The now missing circular oil painting was a copy of The Virgin of the Magnificat, *after Botticelli*
Below: The restored screens passage with Seely and Paget's minstrels' gallery above

⑧ WEST STAIRCASE

Engströmer designed the blackbean veneered sweeping stairs and balustrades on either side of the main entrance, but Seely added the large circular portholes. The large expanse of wall on the west staircase is partially covered by Andrea Piazza's oil painting *The King of Poland Being Received by the Doge of Venice* (c. 1630), which is on loan from the National Gallery of Zimbabwe. Stephen Courtauld admitted the painting was bought 'to fill an unsightly blank piece of staircase wall … it is an amusing rather grey painting of some historical interest but not very much artistic merit'.

⑨ GARTER SUITE

The garter suite is the principal of two guest double bedroom suites. The white painted panelled interior in an early 18th-century style was designed by Seely and Paget. Two divan beds sat on a raised platform with a ceiling pelmet for curtains. The windows contain fragments of 16th-century and later glass collected by Stephen Courtauld. The bedroom now houses a display of objects associated with the Courtaulds and the Army including part of a maid's uniform owned by Ellen Sullivan. Some of the original dining room furniture is also on show (see page 25).

12 STEPHEN COURTAULD'S SUITE

Stephen's suite was designed by Seely to Stephen's requirements. It consists of an aspen-lined bedroom, a walk-in wardrobe and a blue- and green-tiled bathroom. On the side walls of the bedroom is a block-printed wallpaper depicting Kew Gardens made by Sandersons; the coved ceiling represents the sky linking the two landscapes. During repairs straw was found packed within the hollow corridor wall for sound insulation – a technique used at Ealing Studios, where England's first purpose-built sound stage was completed in 1931 (see page 21).

Among the pictures which originally hung in the bedroom were images of people Stephen admired: Beethoven, whose late string quartets were particular favourites; Julius Caesar, revered for his skill as a historian; and Ginie, represented by a photograph of her portrait bust by Lovatelli.

13 PRINCIPAL LANDING

The principal landing incorporates the remains of the 15th-century timber windows of the palace. Prominently hung outside Ginie's bedroom is L Campbell Taylor's impressive 1934 portrait of the Courtaulds with their lemur (see page 1), on loan from a private collection.

Above: Peter Peirano's bedroom, now displayed as a 1960s Royal Army Educational Corps officer's room

Below: Detail of Stephen's bathroom, which was fully tiled by Rust's Vitreous Mosaic Company, London

Right: Stephen's bedroom, 1936. The Kew Gardens wallpaper was rarely produced as the process of hand-printing so many blocks was costly. Sandersons replaced the wallpaper using surviving rolls in the 1960s, but inadvertently transposed the scenes on the two walls

11 OFFICER'S BEDROOM

Peter and Paul Peirano, Ginie's nephews, had adjoining bedrooms sharing a central bathroom. The bedroom occupied by Peter Peirano was occupied in the 1960s by Brigadier Tom Sherry OBE of the Royal Army Educational Corps, and is now displayed as a typical officer's room, complete with an army issue bed and uniforms.

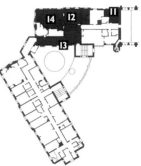

14 VIRGINIA COURTAULD'S BEDROOM

Ginie's suite is much more flamboyant in its design than Stephen's – reflecting both her character and that of Malacrida, the designer. The bedroom is approached via a circular lobby, with three niches for flowers and a curved sliding door.

Ginie's bedroom has the appearance of a primitive temple, with sycamore veneer pilasters and curved walls lined with maple flexwood. A classical shrine once sat within the alcove above the bed, which is flanked by a pair of 1930s walnut and marquetry high-backed chairs. Ginie embroidered the seats with tapestry depictions of a ruined tower and a circular temple in a rural setting.

The room contains classical allusions to three of the four elements: copies of two paintings by Jan Brueghel (1568–1625) represent *Air with Daphne and her Suitor Apollo*, and *Water with Neptune and his Wife Amphitrite*, while fire is alluded to on either side of the reproduction electric fire in the incised depictions of a salamander and a phoenix –

mythical creatures which rose out of the flames. Rectangular recesses at either end of the bedroom contained a dressing table and cupboards. The main light source and the central heating are concealed within the circular ceiling.

Above left: Ginie's bedroom. The flaming torches depicted on the door echo the light brackets around the room, whose crystal figures diffused the light

Above: One of the walnut bedroom chairs with a seat embroidered by Ginie

Left: Ginie outside the drawing room in 1940 with her three dogs Kaïs (Afghan hound), Solfo (giant poodle) – named after one of Stephen's brother Jack's racehorses – and Caesar (Great Dane)

Right: Virginia's bathroom. Above the bath is a statue of Psyche, placed within a gold mosaic niche designed by Malacrida

Below: Detail of the gold-plated lion's-mask spout on Ginie's bath

🔳 VIRGINIA COURTAULD'S BATHROOM

The exotic *en suite* bathroom was also designed by Malacrida. It is the most opulent of all, and accords with *Vogue*'s comment in 1935: 'bathrooms nowadays look more expensive than any rooms in the house'. It has a vaulted ceiling and walls lined with onyx and embellished with black slate disks on to which are set glass spheres. The bath has gold-plated taps and a lion's-mask spout. It sits within a gold mosaic niche containing a statue of the goddess Psyche (the lover of Cupid). This combination of classical statuary and modern design followed the latest Parisian vogue. The original statue was bought in Naples in 1924 by Stephen Courtauld but was later sold; however, an identical one, bought at about the same time by Stephen's sister Catherine, was generously given in 1999 by a member of the family. The bathroom would have been filled with the fragrance of gardenia – Ginie's favourite scent.

16 MAH-JONGG'S QUARTERS

Mah-Jongg or 'Jongy', Ginie's ring-tailed lemur, was bought at Harrods in 1923. An indication of how unusual this exotic pet was is given by Evelyn Waugh, who described another pet lemur in London in 1925 as 'half a cat and half a squirrel and half a monkey'. Jongy was a much-loved pet who accompanied the Courtaulds for 15 years on their travels and changes of residence. But he was infamous for biting people to whom he took a dislike. On the morning of the departure of the 1930–31 British Arctic Air Route Expedition, sponsored by Stephen, the Courtaulds gave a farewell lunch on board their yacht, the *Virginia*; the expedition suffered a severe setback when Jongy bit the hand of Percy Lemon, the expedition's wireless operator, severing an artery. Lemon turned out to be allergic to the iodine which was used to disinfect the wound, and it took him three months to recover.

Jongy's sleeping quarters were centrally heated. The walls were decorated with Madagascan bamboo forest scenes by Gertrude Whinfield, and these have been recreated. A trapdoor leads to the ground-floor flower room.

Left: Jongy in 1936, posing for Country Life *in his decorated and heated sleeping quarters*
Below: A poster for the Ealing Studios' 1949 black comedy Kind Hearts and Coronets. *Stephen was on the board of Ealing Studios*

The windows opposite give a good view of the rock garden beyond the moat, while further along the corridor the window on the left overlooks the glazed dome of the entrance hall and the contrasting 15th-century timber gables.

Ealing Studios

In 1931 Stephen joined the board of Associated Talking Pictures Ltd and Ealing Studios Ltd under the chairmanship of Basil Dean. Over the next 20 years he made a significant personal and financial contribution towards the construction and development of Ealing Studios. Throughout the 1930s the staple Ealing films were comedies starring Gracie Fields and George Formby. In 1938 Stephen enabled Michael Balcon to take charge of the production programme. Balcon oversaw the studio's golden age, developing a distinctive brand of film portraying, in Stephen's words, 'the British ideals and way of living and tradition'. During the war Balcon made morale-boosting and didactic propaganda films such as *The Big Blockade* and *Next of Kin* (both 1942).

The immediate post-war years produced a wide variety of films, including the epic *Scott of the Antarctic* (1948) with a score by Vaughan Williams. Ealing is now best remembered for the comedies which did much to boost public morale in the depressed social conditions of the late 1940s. The most outstanding year was 1949, when three classic comedies were released: *Passport to Pimlico, Kind Hearts and Coronets* (with Alec Guinness playing all eight members of the d'Ascoyne family) and *Whisky Galore* – a title rejected by the American censors so released in America, at Stephen's wry suggestion, as *Tight Little Island*.

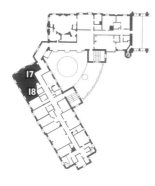

17 VENETIAN SUITE

The Venetian suite was the second of two guest double bedrooms. The dimensions were designed to accommodate joinery removed from Ginie Courtauld's bedroom in Grosvenor Square. These include fragments of 1780s Venetian panelling installed by Malacrida in the 1920s. Malacrida added a screen of three arches on the window wall, and arabesque designs painted on to mirrors. The entrance and cupboard doors are embellished with false book spines. Some of the Courtaulds' home movies are shown in this room.

The bathroom was probably designed by Seely. It is lined with yellow Vitrolite – rolled glass panels manufactured by Pilkington from 1932. Vitrolite was considered at the time to be the ultimate hygienic, easy-clean surface. It was commonly produced in white but yellow was much rarer and a sign of luxury. This suite was occupied by Ginie's mother Rosa when she visited England and the bathroom is the only one in the house to contain a bidet – considered the height of European bathroom chic.

Right: A guest bedroom with built-in walnut furniture by Seely and Paget. Among the books provided for guests were E M Forster's Howard's End *(1910) and Vera Brittain's* Testament of Youth *(1933)*
Below: *The Venetian suite bedroom with mirrored panels by Malacrida, a late 17th-century Italian tabernacle (left) and false book spines on the entrance door (right)*

18 PEAR ROOM

Leading off the lobby is an adjoining dressing room or bedroom designed by Seely, which formed part of the Venetian suite and was known as the Pear Room because of its pear wood fitted furniture. Single rooms such as this provided sufficient accommodation for a comfortable stay but were economical in their use of space. They were designed by Seely, with built-in laminated wood furniture with horizontal lines, reminiscent of cabins in an ocean liner. The bar handles are typical of those favoured by Modern Movement architects in the early 1930s. Beneath the window is a shallow drawer, which acts as a writing desk. All these rooms were heated by an electric fire and equipped with an internal telephone and electric clock.

The secretary's room opposite was occupied by Miss Violet Torckler (known as 'Torckie'). One of the rooms is marked 'Batmen' – a relic, together with the room numbers, of the Army's occupation of Eltham. Beyond the double doors were bedrooms for the ten resident servants: Ginie's maid and three housemaids, Miss Emma Truckle, the cook, two kitchen maids, a butler and two footmen (see plan on the back cover).

The east staircase leads down to the entrance hall. At the bottom, immediately to the left, are double doors leading into the service wing.

19 DINING ROOM

The dining room, designed by Malacrida, exemplifies the sophisticated 'Moderne' style, characterized by geometrical or stylized shapes rather than the organic forms of the earlier Art Nouveau. Malacrida may have been influenced by schemes such as the dining room at the Galeries

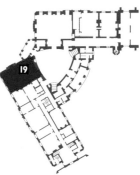

Left: A Christmas dinner party in the dining room at Eltham in 1942. The paintings were removed for the duration of the war. Left to right: Ginie, August Courtauld (Lt RNVR), Edward Keeling (formerly British Consul-General at Tangier), Violet Torckler, Iliffe Cozens (RAF), Mollie Courtauld, Stephen (in Civil Defence uniform), Peter Peirano, Sir George Binney (Lt Commander RNVR), Major George Courtauld (Stephen's cousin and director of personnel in the Special Operations Executive) and his wife Claudine

Below: John Crome's dramatic oil painting The Lime Kiln, c.1805–6, which hangs in the dining room

Lafayette, shown at the seminal Paris 'Exposition des Arts Décoratifs' of 1925, from which the term 'Art Deco' was later coined. The design relies on contrasting tones and textures for effect. The walls are lined with paper-thin bird's-eye maple flexwood, as are the ceiling cove and picture frames. In dramatic contrast the recessed central portion of the ceiling is covered entirely in aluminium leaf on a blue background, with built-in concealed lighting to make the metal shimmer at night; around the perimeter are rose-shaped ornaments (*paterae*) covered in aluminium. A comparable ceiling of the same period can be found in the ballroom of the Park Lane Hotel, Piccadilly. The floor has a black marble perimeter surrounding a reproduction buff carpet with a brown and black border. The fireplace consists of polished, ribbed aluminium panels surrounding the original electric fire, which still retains its imitation logs illuminated by electric bulbs. It has a black Belgian marble surround inlaid with a Greek key pattern in mica. This classical motif, which is repeated on the ebonized doors and side tables, was often used in the 1930s. Two Ancient Greek amphorae (jars) stood on the sideboard (the ones on display are modern copies), and the whole effect suggests the atrium of a Roman house. The built-in cabinets have glass shelves and mirror backs, which are typical Art Deco features; they contained a selection of ancient Persian and

Chinese pottery and porcelain. (The ceramics currently on display give a sense of the colours and designs of the originals.) The striking doors feature animals and birds drawn at London Zoo by Narini, according to *Country Life*, and applied as ivory-coloured raised decoration. The significance of the choice of subjects is not known.

The furniture was reproduced from photographs and descriptions, including the dining chairs with pink leather upholstery (rose pink was considered at the time to be 'an ideal colour for setting off ladies' dresses to the best advantage'). The original dining table and chairs were subsequently rediscovered. The choice of pictures – all landscapes – evidently formed part of the original plan for the room, since the frames are specifically designed for this room. Reading clockwise from just to the left of the entrance

doors, they were: *The Lime Kiln* by John Crome; *View near Keswick* by Peter de Wint (missing); *Lake Nemi* by Richard Wilson; *The River Brent* and *Bonneville, Savoy*, both by J M W Turner; and *The Falls at Inverary* by Patrick Naysmith (missing). One of the Turners has been reproduced with the help of the National Gallery, London. The original Crome was purchased with the assistance of the Art Fund.

In addition to the electric fire, the room was heated by hot-water pipes embedded in the central ceiling panel. On the end wall are a circular barometer and electric clock, while on the wall opposite the fireplace is a loudspeaker, which was wired to the record cabinet in the great hall corridor.

20 SERVICE WING

The door to the left of the loudspeaker leads into a servery. It is lined with white Vitrolite with a green band. On the left is a silver safe, which originally contained a 1935 silver service commissioned for the house, and over 60 pieces of 18th-century, Courtauld-made silver (the Courtaulds were originally goldsmiths and silversmiths). The servery contains the food lift connecting to the first floor. At the far end is a lobby leading to the kitchen

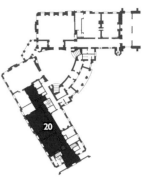

(now the tea room). Most of the kitchen fittings are now gone but they included early 'Savestain' steel sinks and two Jackson's electric cookers. English Heritage has attempted to restore some of the room's original character. The shop beyond the kitchen was once the servants' hall.

The basement contains the motor for the vacuum cleaner (see page 47), Stephen's photographic dark room, a games room and billiards room. There are also cellars surviving from the 19th-century house, Eltham Court, which were formed out of the palace remains. The basement has a reinforced concrete ceiling and the cellars were used as air-raid shelters throughout the war.

Left: The billiards room in the basement. The mural on the far wall was commissioned by Stephen from Mary Adshead (1904–95) for the music room at 47 Grosvenor Square
Below: The original dining room furniture on display in the Garter suite

Facing page: A view from the dining room, past the doors with Narini's applied lacquer animals, into the entrance hall

The Discovery of the Dining Room Table and Chairs

In 2000 a remarkable discovery was made of the original dining room table and chairs, designed by Malacrida. While waiting to see the doctor, the retired property store manager of Pinewood Studios was reading a 1999 copy of *World of Interiors* magazine, which featured an article on Eltham's restoration. Thinking the dining room furniture looked familiar, he tore out the page and returned to Pinewood, where he found the furniture in the store; it had been modified for use in films over a number of years. He contacted English Heritage and the furniture was subsequently purchased for Eltham. Some of the furniture is now on display in the Garter suite. The pink leather had been dyed brown by Pinewood Studios, but the modern reproductions proved to be remarkably accurate.

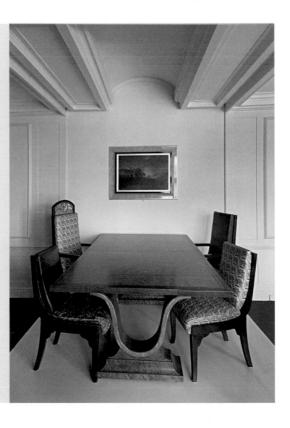

Tour of the Gardens

Stephen and Ginie conceived ambitious plans for their new gardens at Eltham. Today they are a rare and very fine example of a 1930s garden that is open to the public. The fact that they incorporate elements of the medieval palace adds a further intriguing dimension. The tour begins with the remains of the medieval palace: the north bridge, moated walls and buttresses, and the exposed remains of the queen's apartments. The Courtaulds created a variety of garden features, including a rock garden, formal rose gardens and a series of garden 'rooms' typical of the period. English Heritage has also introduced some Art Deco-inspired contemporary planting in the south moat designed by Isabelle van Groeningen.

FOLLOWING THE TOUR

This tour begins by the turning circle outside the entrance to the Courtauld house, from where visitors can see the remains of the royal palace. Visitors then go past the squash court to the south garden at the foot of the south moat wall, and then on to the garden rooms and the north moat. The tour ends by the house in the triangular garden.

Left: Richard II's 14th-century moat bridge with the weeping willow in the foreground
Below: The spout of a jug dating from about 1300, found in Bishop Bek's cellar during excavations in 1976

Facing page: Queen Isabella's 1315 stone south moat wall in front of part of the great hall and the Courtauld bedroom wing

REMAINS OF THE ROYAL PALACE

Eltham became one of the largest and most frequented royal palaces in the country. It was Edward IV's favourite residence after Westminster.

Beyond the service wing are the remains of the brick inner gatehouse. The north stone bridge was built by Richard II in 1396. It had a drawbridge at the near end, which was discovered during repairs in 1912. The stone coping (protective capping) is thought to have been salvaged from the crenellated parapet on the great hall, which was removed in the 19th century.

The medieval inner court (see the plan on page 42) lies beneath the Courtaulds' turning circle. The Caen stone string-course on the great hall, beneath the 20th-century parapet, is enriched with 15th-century grotesque heads. The entrance to the great hall is decorated with restored 'rose en soleil' emblems of Edward IV in the spandrels over the door.

The turning circle and the area around the squash court are rich in the remains of the medieval palace. At the far right, behind the Italian ornamental well-head (added by the Courtaulds), are the exposed remains of angular towers of stone and yellow brick, probably part of the works to the moated manor house by Anthony Bek, bishop of Durham (a powerful bishop, soldier and statesman) in 1300. The lawn was partially excavated in the 1950s and 1970s to reveal the remains of Bek's work – a great hall floored with tiles dating to about 1300 and a vaulted cellar, both of which have since been reburied. Exposed to view are the remains of the west range of the palace's royal apartments, the king's to the south and the queen's to the north, mostly of brick and probably built by Edward IV. Also excavated but now reburied are the remains of Henry VIII's chapel, dating from the 1520s, and a gallery to his apartments. The brick remains of the outer moat wall are part of Elizabeth I's and James I's refronting, behind which was a corridor whose bay windows gave magnificent views across to London (see the reconstruction on page 28).

The brick gable ends of the great hall are evidence of Elizabeth I's repairs in 1574. Excavations of the area beyond the Courtaulds' squash court in 1952 uncovered some of the arched buttresses inserted to support Bishop Bek's moat wall, and the new stone outer wall built in 1315 for Queen Isabella, wife of Edward II, by three London masons. Structural faults led to the masons being charged with poor workmanship. This was upheld by a jury and the masons were imprisoned, but they were subsequently released to enable them to demolish and rebuild their work.

The buttressed south-facing side of the great hall, overlooking the former kitchen courtyard, is constructed of roughly dressed, coursed Kentish ragstone. Originally, the carved work was executed in Caen stone. Beneath the south lawn are the buried remains of the kitchen and other service buildings and apartments, together with Henry VIII's drainage system (see page 41). The timber central bridge over the south moat was added by Seely and Paget on brick footings, which probably supported a now-lost 1580s bridge. The retaining walls to the moat on the south and east sides are on the alignment of the early 14th-century stone walls, with extensive brick alterations surviving from the mid-16th century onwards. The two brick-built buttresses on the south side are probably of mid-18th-century date. The ragged top courses of brick were added by Seely and Paget to be in sympathy with the Tudor work. On the west side at the southern end, brick diaper work to the bases of five bay windows dates from the rebuilding of the sovereign's apartments by Elizabeth I. Further north the rebuilding in brick of the queen's apartment bay windows by James I in 1603 represents the last major building work undertaken while Eltham was still a royal palace.

A Tudor brick drain descends into the south moat, which is now reached via steps and a reset, concave-moulded, narrow stone arch, probably of late 15th- or early 16th-century date. Above was a passage which led from the king's lodgings to Henry VIII's privy bridge. In the 15th century the privy garden lay to the south-east of the moat. This was greatly enhanced by Henry VIII, who laid out hedges, arbours and a high wooden fence for privacy. There was an interlaced alley of plum and cherry trees to shade archers shooting at the nearby butts. Beyond the privy garden, the palace was encircled by three parks used for hunting.

Above: Diaper brickwork decorating the new front of the sovereign's lodgings, rebuilt for Elizabeth I in the 1580s
Left: One of the 56 arch buttresses added in 1315 to support Bek's failing moat wall. Seven have been exposed in excavations, but the ground between the old and new moat walls would originally have been covered over
Below left: The south elevation of the great hall. The door leads into the screens passage. The roughly dressed Kentish ragstone belongs to Edward IV's work but the higher masonry repairs are dated 1912

Facing page: A reconstruction of Eltham Palace in about 1604, based primarily on two surveys by Thorpe
A The outer gatehouse
B Outer court flanked by service buildings
C Lord Chancellor's lodgings
D North bridge
E Courtiers' lodgings
F Inner court
G Chapel
H Queen's apartments
I King's apartments
J Great hall
K Service courtyards
L Privy bridge

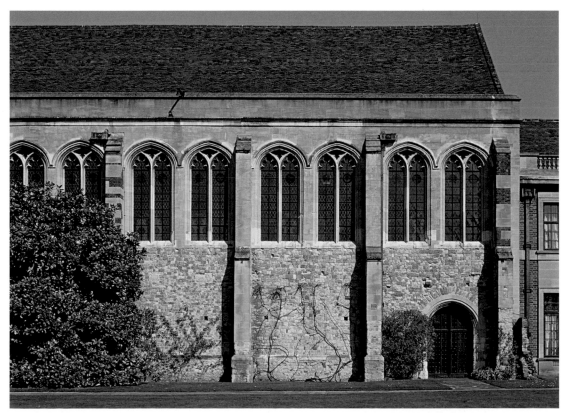

Right: Part of Seely and Paget's scheme for the gardens, 1934. Some of the proposals were not carried out, such as the Chinese bridge over the east moat, while the sunken rose garden was simplified in execution

Below: St George by Alfred Hardiman, outside the squash court. This bronze statue was commissioned in 1926 by Stephen Courtauld for the squash court niche in Carlos Place, behind 47 Grosvenor Square in London

DESIGN OF THE COURTAULD GARDENS

Before the Courtaulds could start work on the gardens, some of the medieval retaining walls had to be rebuilt – especially on the east side – and the moat was partially re-excavated and flooded. An initial, very formal Beaux Arts design was imposed on the site by Andrew Mawson and Partners, and exhibited at the Chelsea Flower Show in 1935. But Stephen and Ginie wanted to feature a variety of garden styles fashionable in the 1930s. Seely and Paget produced a plan which was further revised in consultation with John Gilmour, assistant director of Kew Gardens since 1931. The scheme that was eventually adopted featured a progression of garden areas, similar to contemporary gardens at Sissinghurst, Kent, and Great Dixter, Sussex. The planting was probably implemented by a firm of nurserymen assisted by the Courtaulds' gardener, James Blackman.

The Courtaulds kept most of the existing trees, but added ornamental plantations, shrubberies and specimen trees – some of which were gifts from members of the royal family. In addition they laid out new garden areas. They were keen

horticulturalists: Stephen had a passion for orchids, which he raised in the glasshouses, and Ginie for roses, which she obtained from the celebrated Sam McGredy nurseries at Portadown, Northern Ireland. (The Courtaulds later created a red rose in their Zimbabwean home called 'Virginia Courtauld'.) The 1930s planting is a mixture of informality in the Japanese rockery east of the moat, and formality on the west side in the rose garden, with its sunken pond and a series of enclosed rooms. Much of the structure and some of the original planting of the Courtauld era still survive, and have been uncovered by English Heritage's gradual restoration of the gardens to their 1930s appearance.

SQUASH COURT

The turning circle contains a large lime tree planted by the Courtaulds. The grey brick building with red brick arches was Seely and Paget's squash court. In a brick niche is an elegant bronze statue of St George by Alfred Hardiman (1891–1949), dated 1930. Originally commissioned by Stephen for the Grosvenor Square property, the statue was relocated to Eltham in 1936. St George is depicted as a Greek warrior and was originally partly gilded. The shield is decorated with animals and birds representing countries of the British Empire.

In the Courtauld era the area between the squash court and the retaining wall of the moat contained a formal garden of oval beds, preserved from the garden of the 19th-century house on the site. In the middle was a sundial set on to a baluster (pillar) from Waterloo Bridge, which was demolished between 1935 and 1936. This garden was removed when excavations were carried out in the 1950s.

SOUTH GARDEN AND MOAT

The holly hedge at the west end of the south garden was an important addition to shelter the trees from the prevailing wind. Notable trees planted by the Courtaulds include the magnificent *Catalpa bignonioides* (Indian bean tree), *Liriodendron tulipifera* (tulip tree), *Juglans regia* (walnut) and *Laurus nobilis* (bay). Rectangular beds at the top of the moat wall were planted with bedding tulips in spring and dahlias in summer. The timber bridge over the moat is framed by *Senecio greyii* and yucca, both popular in the 1930s.

Left: The south moat wall, framed by Isabelle van Groeningen's herbaceous border, and Seely and Paget's timber bridge

Below: The herbaceous border, photographed in the 1930s. Taller varieties, such as delphiniums, were planted at the back, in smaller and more irregular groupings than might be expected today

The orangery adjoined the south side of the squash court. This was used to display exotic plants grown in the glasshouses. To the east a fine *Magnolia grandiflora* sits between two of the great hall buttresses. The Courtauld south front is set back from the face of the great hall so as not to interfere visually with the medieval masonry. This front contains the principal rooms including the drawing room, while the sculpture above is *Apollo*, god of the arts (with a lyre under his arm), by H Carlton Attwood. Climbers and shrubs were trained tightly against the wall.

The long mixed herbaceous border at the foot of the south moat wall was replanted in 2000 as part of a new garden designed by Isabelle van Groeningen. The tall plants, such as the miscanthus and molinia grasses, delphiniums, eupatoriums and

late compositae, all play a vital role in providing the necessary height and volume that fit the scale and solidity of the imposing moat walls and the brick piers of the bridge. The regular repetition of certain key plants such as *Nepeta racemosa* 'Walker's Low' and *Sedum spectabile* establishes a basic pattern, providing a pleasing unity and rhythm. This is reinforced more subtly with other genera using varying cultivars – hemerocallis, peony, poppy and delphinium – to provide both an element of repetition and variety.

The gardeners manage the far moat bank and parkland as a meadow, as it was in the Courtaulds' time, by taking off a hay crop in July, and the 'aftermath' is then mown until Christmas (mowing substitutes for grazing). This has encouraged the development of the seed bank of wild flowers which had lain dormant during the decades when the bank was close mown like a lawn. In spring the bank is now covered with primroses, wood anemone, dog's mercury, and native bluebells, which are an indicator of ancient woodland. Each spring there is a greater diversity: oxlips, for example, now flower profusely and snakeshead fritillaries have begun to colonize in wetter springs. A summer meadow is also beginning to develop.

Two modern curved seats in green oak in the moat are enclosed by clipped evergreens.

Right: The sunken rose garden, which was created by Stephen and Ginie
Below: Stephen's seven-seater Streamline car in Grosvenor Square, 1931

SUNKEN ROSE GARDEN

The rectangular rose garden was created by Stephen and Ginie. It is enclosed by hedges and the moat wall. At the centre of the pool was a bronze fountain of a boy and fish, bought by Stephen in Florence; this was a copy of Verrocchio's late 15th-century sculpture in the Palazzo Vecchio. (The fountain is a gift from the late Peter Peirano and is currently awaiting conservation.) The pool is planted with water lilies and surrounded by four Irish yews, rose beds and a low brick wall topped by a lavender hedge.

GARDEN ROOMS

Two consecutive garden rooms beyond the sunken garden are divided by shrubbery, including *Viburnum x burkwoodii*, bred as recently as 1924, and *Poncirus trifoliata* (a hardy citrus relative). The shrubs, including multi-stemmed trees of *Ligustrum lucidum* from China, provide shade for the borders on the outer edges containing winter and spring planting. Other shrubs in this area now include *Daphne bholua*, *Stachyurus praecox*, *Edgeworthia*, *Osmanthus yunnanensis*, *Philadelphus delavayi*, and a number of deutzias, hydrangeas and tree peonies. The Lady Sudley apple in the first room is a survivor from the former Victorian planting.

The rooms terminate in a formal pool of water at the end of the moat, with a fountain as its focal point. The pool is partially enclosed by tree and shrub planting.

The chauffeur's block and garage beyond the modern fence were designed by Seely and Paget. The roof can be glimpsed to the left of the pool beyond the trees. Stephen owned at least one Rolls Royce, but he particularly liked Mercedes cars. Ginie also owned a Mercedes in the 1930s. In 1931 Stephen bought one of the revolutionary and sensational Dennis Burney Streamlines (Stephen and his brother Jack were both directors of the company). Among the features were hydraulic brakes, independent suspension and a rear engine, giving a smooth, quiet ride even at 80 miles per

Left: The sunken rose garden, 1936. The pots were probably supplied by an art pottery such as Compton Pottery, near Guildford

Below: Detail of the unicorn supporter from the Palace of Westminster, flanking a repositioned 15th-century window in the north moat wall

hour. The seven-seater car was expensive by 1931 standards, costing £1500 (about the price of a four-bedroomed detached house in Eltham at the time). Herbert Moore, Stephen's chauffeur since before the First World War, remained until his retirement in 1947. There is a story of 'Old' Moore driving to Istanbul to meet the Courtaulds in their yacht as prearranged. On arrival, Stephen told him there had been a change of plan, and Moore promptly began the long journey back to England.

NORTH MOAT AND EAST GARDEN

Beyond the north stone bridge is a weeping willow on an island, fashionable in the 1930s. Within the moat wall beyond the bridge is a stone window moved here from elsewhere in the palace. The lion and unicorn supporters were salvaged from Charles Barry's Palace of Westminster during restoration work in 1935 and were obtained by Stephen's friend the MP Rab Butler. From the top of the stepped path within the bank is a fine view of Seely and Paget's loggia and east wing, the latter featuring sculptures representing *Domesticity* by H Carlton Attwood. The eastern ridge is lined with trees and shrub planting. Notable plants are *Cornus mas* (Cornelian cherry) bearing small yellow flowers in winter and small red berries in late

summer, and the strawberry tree *Arbutus unedo*, an evergreen with lily-of-the-valley flowers and strawberry-shaped fruit in autumn. Nearer the car park was the former tiltyard of the palace. The timber-clad pavilion was adapted by Seely and Paget from Victorian stables to serve the Courtaulds' former hard and grass tennis courts. Beyond the locked pedestrian gate is the Courtaulds' brick quadrant rose garden, which was originally laid out in a single colour, such as the magenta Glory of Rome supplied by McGredy.

In the 1930s the area now occupied by the car park comprised a large rectangular utility area, with glasshouses and sheds built for the Courtaulds. They included two orchid houses as well as a carnation house, peach house and vinery. Orchids were Stephen's particular passion and he received awards from the Royal Horticultural Society for their propagation.

Further along the moat bank, past a flowering tulip tree (*Liriodendron tulipifera*), there is another fine view of the Courtauld wing. The hedged former swimming pool was filled in in 1967; the octagonal timber changing room was moved from its original position and is now situated in the Cutting Garden. (By 1935 a swimming pool was considered indispensable for a country house.)

Right: The Japanese rock garden seen from the loggia terrace
Below: One of Gilbert Ledward's reliefs on the loggia depicting Ginie's gardening interests

Facing page: The pergola, covered in wisteria. The 18th-century Ionic columns were salvaged from the Bank of England when it was controversially rebuilt by Sir Herbert Baker between 1925 and 1939

ROCK GARDEN

Water was reintroduced in the eastern moat by the Courtaulds in a serpentine shape, edged in concrete. The furthest bank was laid out as a rock garden using water-washed limestone; a Japanese maple, a pine and a juniper remain from the original design. Rock gardens had become popular by the 1930s, partly due to Reginald Farrer's book *The English Rock Garden* (1919), of which Stephen owned a copy. A water feature here comprises a series of pools and cascades running down to the moat. Ginie bought a pair of black-necked Patagonian swans which bred successfully in the moat. The exotic black and white birds appealed to her, and the idea of swans – which are royal birds – may have been inspired by a possible derivation of the place-name Eltham from the Anglo-Saxon word *elfetu*, meaning 'swan'.

LOGGIA, PERGOLA AND TRIANGULAR GARDEN

Steps in a bastion made by Seely and Paget lead to the loggia and pergola. The loggia is embellished with four reliefs carved by Gilbert Ledward, depicting some of the interests of Stephen and Virginia Courtauld: gardening and sports framing idealized formal portraits, and sailing and mountaineering. The pergola is covered in wisteria in spring. The supporting stone Ionic columns were salvaged from the Bank of England in the 1930s; they are probably late 18th-century in date and by Robert Taylor, the bank's architect. A mulberry tree remains from the Victorian garden.

An awkward narrow corner between the service wing and the retaining wall is filled by a triangular kitchen garden. A brick lattice pattern separates formal blocks of modern planting.

History

Eltham was originally a moated manor house, built by Anthony Bek, bishop of Durham, in the late 13th century. It was enlarged by successive monarchs from Edward II to James I, after which it fell into decline, with Edward IV's magnificent great hall being used as a barn. Stephen Courtauld purchased a 99-year lease of the site in 1933. He restored the great hall and added a modern house, designed by Seely and Paget. The Courtaulds left after the war and the palace was subsequently occupied by various Army education units. English Heritage took over its management in 1995 and restored and refurnished the opulent 1930s interiors and gardens.

Left: Bishop Odo blessing a meal, in a scene from the Bayeux Tapestry. The manor of Eltham belonged to him in 1086

Below: Floor tiles from Bek's great hall dating from about 1300. They are identical to tiles found at Lesnes Abbey near Erith, Kent, and were probably made by the same tilers

Facing page: A 15th-century portrait of Edward IV (r.1461–83), who built the great hall at Eltham

THE GROWTH OF THE ROYAL PALACE

Anglo-Saxon pottery has been found at Eltham, but otherwise little is known of any settlement here until the Domesday survey of 1086, when the manor of Eltham is recorded as being in the possession of Odo, bishop of Bayeux, the half-brother of William the Conqueror (r.1066–87). The estate changed hands several times until 1295 when the manor was acquired by Bishop Bek. According to Robert of Graystones, a contemporary chronicler, Bek 'most elaborately built the manor of Eltham', implying an impressive structure. The extent of Bek's work is not fully known, but he constructed a defensive wall of rubble-stone, flint and brick around the moat, with octagonal bastions. A cellar and the remains of Bek's great hall with an octagonal stone hearth and elaborate tiled floor were excavated in the 1970s. The hall was oriented north–south and lay to the west of the modern turning circle. A timber drawbridge, probably on the site of the present north bridge, led to the manor house. Bek also created a hunting park to the west of the moat, which was later known as the Old, or Middle Park.

Edward I (r.1272–1307) and his son the prince of Wales (the future Edward II) frequently stayed at Eltham, and in 1305 Bek presented the manor to the prince, although Bek retained it until his death here in 1311.

Edward II (r.1307–27) granted the manor to Isabella, his queen. Considerable improvements were made, including enlarging the moated site between 1315 and 1316 by buttressing Bek's wall and constructing a new 12ft (3.7m) high wall beyond it, with the space in between filled with rubble. Excavations have revealed the buttressing to Bek's wall and the new outer wall near the Courtaulds' squash court. The existing moat walls are on the same alignment as the 1315–16 walls, although much altered with 15th-century and later brickwork. Edward and Isabella's second son John was born at Eltham in 1316 and was baptized in the chapel here. He was known as John of Eltham, a fact that might account for the palace erroneously being referred to from at least the early 18th century as King John's Court.

By the early 14th century, Eltham had become one of the largest and most frequented royal residences in the country. Edward III (r.1327–77)

*Right: Edward III granting the
Black Prince the principality
of Aquitaine, from a
contemporary manuscript.
The king spent much of his
youth at Eltham*

*Below: Roger Mortimer, 4th
earl of March, in his garter
robes, c.1440–50. Edward III
established the Order of the
Garter in 1348 and held
a tournament at Eltham
shortly after*

spent much of his youth here and frequently
visited Eltham as king. He established the Order of
the Garter – the oldest surviving order of chivalry
in Europe – in 1348. A royal wardrobe account
includes 12 garters of blue embroidered in gold
and silk with the order's motto 'Honi soit qui mal y
pense' ('Let shame be to him who thinks this evil'),
which were supplied for a joust at Eltham in the
late 1340s. Tournaments probably took place in
the outer court until the tiltyard was created in

1517 beyond the moat to the north-east. Extensive
works were undertaken for Edward III in the
1350s, including further alterations to the moat
walls, and the construction of a new drawbridge
and service buildings, such as a stone great kitchen
and a new 'roasting house'. New royal lodgings on
the east side of the site featured a bathroom with
a tiled floor and glazed windows for the king.
There are references to chapels for the king and
queen and to a garden with vines, while beyond
the moat, to the south and east, further land was
enclosed with a ditch and hedging between 1367
and 1368 as part of what was later known as the
Great Park. Later, Richard II (r.1377–99) and his
successors created the Lee, New or Horn Park
to the west beyond the Middle Park. Including
Bek's 'Old' Park, the three parks comprised almost
1,300 acres (525ha).

Richard II created a garden on the south side
of the palace beyond the moat in the 1380s 'for
the king and queen to have dinner there in the
summer time', as well as a dancing chamber and a
new bathhouse within the king's apartments. He
also rebuilt the timber north bridge in stone.
Henry IV (r.1399–1413) spent 10 of his 13
Christmases as king at Eltham. He altered the
planning of the palace in about 1400 by building
himself a new set of timber-framed apartments
with stone chimney-stacks on the west side.
Henry's chamber contained elaborate stained glass
depicting his badge and portraits of various saints
by the London glazier William Burgh. A set of
two-storey lodgings was also built for the queen.
In 1445 new buildings were erected for Margaret
of Anjou, bride of Henry VI (r.1422–61), including
a new hall and service rooms.

Eltham was Edward IV's favourite residence
apart from Westminster. Roger Appleton was
appointed 'master and surveyor of the repair and
building of the king's manor of Eltham' with James
Hatfield as clerk of works. They opened up the
courtyard by removing Bek's hall and building the
magnificent surviving great hall at right angles to it
between 1475 and 1480. Edward IV also built a
service range – of which the three timber gables
survive – and a new, separate, brick range of royal
lodgings on the west side. One of the most lavish
feasts ever held in the palace was given for some
2,000 people at Christmas 1482 during Edward IV
and his queen's last visit to Eltham.

Left: An early 20th-century painting by F Cadogan Cowper in the Palace of Westminster of Erasmus and Thomas More visiting the children of Henry VII at Eltham in 1499
Below: A 15th-century portrait of the poet Geoffrey Chaucer. As clerk of works to Richard II, he visited Eltham
Below left: Jean Froissart, who visited Eltham in 1395, presents a book to Richard II, from a 15th-century manuscript

Famous Visitors to Eltham

Eltham continued to be frequented by the court until well into the 16th century, and during this time many international statesmen were entertained here. In 1356 John II of France was defeated at the battle of Poitiers (the most decisive English victory of the Hundred Years War) and captured. He visited Eltham briefly in 1360 on his way back to France, but in 1364 he returned to voluntary exile in England following the refusal of the duke of Anjou to honour the terms of his parole. Edward III received King John amid two days of 'great dancing and caroling'. John was accompanied by Jean Froissart, who subsequently recorded the event in his lively *Chronicles*. Froissart returned to Eltham in 1395 to present Richard II with a collection of his poems. In 1385 Leo V, the exiled king of Armenia, came to Richard's court at Eltham to seek support in regaining his throne from the Turks. Five years later Richard's clerk of works, the poet Chaucer, was mugged twice, possibly on his way to the palace, and lost £40 of official funds as well as his horse. Henry IV received Manuel Palaeologus, the Byzantine emperor, at Eltham at Christmas 1400, where the entertainment included a mumming (a mime) performed by 12 London aldermen and a parade and jousting tournament in the outer court on New Year's day. In 1416 Sigismund, Holy Roman Emperor, discussed church affairs here with Henry V (r. 1413–22) and forged an alliance with him. One of the most charming accounts concerns Prince Henry (later Henry VIII), much of whose boyhood was spent at Eltham. Here, in 1499, the precocious nine-year-old prince met the Dutch philosopher Erasmus whom he embarrassed by challenging him to write a poem. Within three days Erasmus duly produced a verse in praise of England, Henry VII, and the princes Arthur and Henry.

Chaucer was mugged twice, possibly on his way to Eltham, and lost money and his horse

Above: A portrait of Cardinal Wolsey, who in 1525 drew up the Eltham Ordinances at the palace, which aimed to control access to the king
Above right: Oak panelling from Eltham Palace, dating from about 1530 and possibly originally in Henry VIII's new chapel at Eltham
Below: A 16th-century portrait of Henry VIII by Holbein. The king spent much of his boyhood at Eltham

HENRY VII AND HENRY VIII

During Henry VII's reign (1485–1509) the palace served as a nursery for the princes and princesses, although it was still visited by the court. Henry VII 'set up the faire front over the moat', according to a 1570 account. If true, this may refer to alterations to the west front, which housed the royal

apartments. In July 1517 a tiltyard was laid out at Eltham to the east of the palace, probably to avoid the inconvenience of preparing the outer court for each joust. By the 1520s extensive works were in progress for Henry VIII (r.1509–47), including new king's lodgings, alterations to the queen's lodgings and the construction of a new brick-built chapel similar in size to Edward IV's great hall and located in the courtyard (within what is now the turning circle). The chapel was elaborately decorated: gilt lead leaves were found in excavations in the choir, while ornate Renaissance oak panelling (now at the Greenwich Heritage Centre, Woolwich) was reputedly removed from the palace – possibly from the chapel – after the Civil Wars. The density of building within the walls of the moat left little space for gardens, and a new privy garden was constructed to the south and east. This included paths and bowers, a bowling green and archery butts.

On Christmas Eve 1515 Cardinal Wolsey took the oath of office of lord chancellor in the chapel at Eltham before the king. In 1525 Wolsey drew up the Eltham Ordinances here. These reforming regulations of the royal household aimed to reduce waste. Wolsey also sought to control access to the king. The fact that the ordinances carry the name of Eltham is an indication of the palace's continuing importance at this period. Eltham was one of only six palaces large enough to accommodate and feed the entire court of 800 or more people. During the 1530s, however,

Henry VIII increasingly embellished Hampton Court, as the focus of the court moved westwards. Henry was the last monarch to spend substantial amounts of time at Eltham. Greenwich was more convenient and accessible from Westminster by river, and the hunting that Eltham's three parks provided was fairly easily reached from there.

ELIZABETH AND THE EARLY STUARTS

Queen Elizabeth I (r.1558–1603) visited Eltham only occasionally. In the 1580s the two south timber bridges were rebuilt, and a new west front made for the sovereign's apartments at the south-west using diapered brick and Oxfordshire stone. This included a battlemented parapet and one bay window supported by a central, angular pier. In 1603, however, James I (r.1603–25) found the palace 'farre in decay' and substantial repairs were undertaken and a new brick and stone façade was added to the queen's apartments at the north-west end, incorporating a brick range of five-sided bay windows and chimneybreasts, which can be seen from the west moat. The lodgings were connected to a recreational gallery giving spectacular views across London. James I also improved the approach to the palace by refronting the two bays on the east side of the porter's lodge to match those on the west, as shown in the Buck view of 1735 (see page 43).

Charles I (r.1625–49) was the last king to visit the palace. During the 17th century its buildings were poorly maintained. Between 1617 and 1618, and again between 1631 and 1632, there are reports of parts of the palace collapsing.

Left: A portrait of Queen Elizabeth I made in the late 1580s, attributed to George Gower. Elizabeth built a new west front for her apartments at Eltham in the 1580s
Below: Part of the Tudor drainage system beneath the south lawn, with a panel commemorating the investigation of the tunnel in 1834

Tudor Sanitation

A regular water supply was needed for food preparation and sanitation for large numbers of people at the palace. This was initially supplied by wells, but in 1482 a brick conduit – which still survives – was built about 0.6 miles to the east of the palace. Water was carried in lead or hollow elm pipes to the kitchens, lodgings (including the bathhouse) and laundry.

An intricate network of underground tunnels at Eltham has given rise to rumours of secret passages leading to Greenwich Palace and underground stables. In fact it was part of Henry VIII's drainage system which conveyed foul water from the kitchens. Other brick tunnels were connected to the garderobes (latrines), which were regularly flushed with clean water, while pits collected solid matter which was periodically shovelled out by highly paid royal servants known as 'gong scourers', after one of the many Tudor names for a latrine.

**Survey of Eltham Palace
by John Thorpe, c.1604**

A Bek turrets, c.1300

B Moat wall, 1315

C Courtiers' lodgings,
1350s

D North bridge, 1396

E Great hall, c.1480

F Kitchens and service
buildings, c.1480

G Chapel, 1520s

H Sovereign's
apartments, 1580s

I Queen's apartments,
1603–4

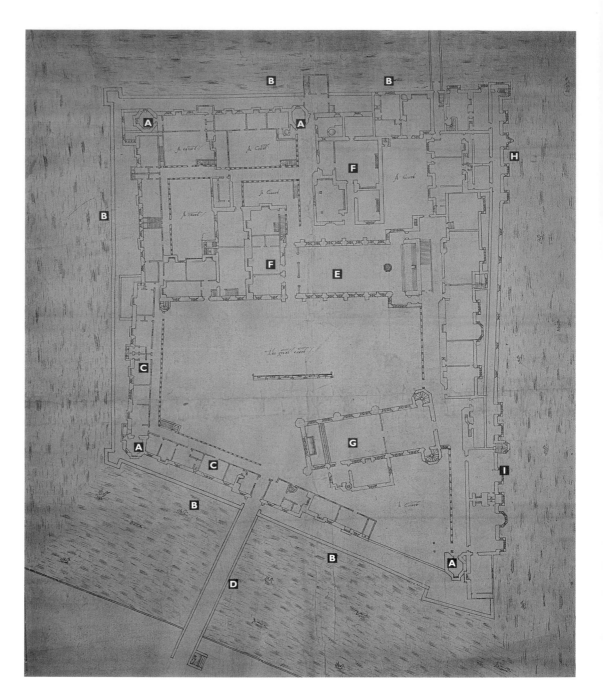

THE PALACE AT ITS PEAK

Two ground-floor surveys of Eltham Palace by John Thorpe made in 1590 and about 1604 depict the palace complex at its fullest development. The area occupied by the palace at its widest point was some 1,000ft by 500ft (305m x 152m), which far exceeded that of Hampton Court. The 1604 plan above shows the north bridge at the bottom with the gatehouse and porter's lodge at the inner end. Bishop Bek's angular turrets are enveloped by the 1315 walls. Around the Great Court (where Thorpe positioned his scale bar) are timber lean-to galleries which gave covered access to the main residences: courtiers' lodgings on the north and east (left of the bridge), and the queen's apartments on the west side of the courtyard, with a series of bay windows built by James I between 1603 and 1604. The king's apartments at the top right-hand corner adjoin a small bridge leading into the privy garden. The range projecting into the great court is Henry VIII's chapel. Above it is Edward IV's great hall leading to the royal apartments. Behind the hall are the kitchens within a series of smaller service courts.

THE CIVIL WARS

In 1648 Parliamentary troops were quartered at Eltham to quench a revolt in Kent, and much of the palace and the royal parks were ransacked. During the Civil Wars a Parliamentary survey of 1649 concluded that Eltham was 'much out of repair, and soe not tenantable'. All the deer in the parks had been killed and all the good timber within the parks was felled for the use of the Navy. The manor was sold in 1651 to the Parliamentarian Colonel Nathaniel Rich, who demolished many buildings and stripped the lead off the great hall roof. When the diarist John Evelyn visited Eltham in 1656 he lamented 'both the palace and chapel [are] in miserable ruins, the noble wood and park destroyed by Rich the Rebel'.

RESTORATION TO THE CROWN

At the restoration of the monarchy in 1660 the palace reverted to the Crown, but the remaining buildings – notably the hall and chapel – were in ruins. Sir John Shaw, who had advanced money to Charles II while he was in exile, leased the manor in 1663, but he never lived at the palace. Instead he employed the architect Hugh May to build Eltham Lodge in the former Great Park (now the Royal Blackheath Golf Club House).

THE PALACE UNDER THREAT

During the 18th century the palace remains were put to agricultural use. The great hall trusses were exposed to the elements before the roof was tiled and the hall used as a barn. The window tracery gradually decayed and many of the windows were partially bricked up. The palace site deteriorated into a picturesque ruin, attracting artists and antiquarians who clambered over the stonework and explored the tunnels. Artists such as Paul Sandby, Thomas Girtin and J M W Turner depicted the ruins, while detailed architectural drawings were published in 1828 by H Dunnage and C Laver in *Plans, Elevations … of the Great Hall of … Eltham.*

In 1827 Jeffry Wyatville, architect to George IV (r. 1820–30), announced his intention of dismantling the roof and re-erecting it as part of the new St George's Hall at Windsor Castle. This proposal was abandoned, but later in the year a gale damaged the roof and the Office of Woods

Above: Portrait of John Evelyn, 1648, by Robert Walker. Evelyn was shocked at the state of the palace when he visited in 1656
Left: The earliest surviving image of the west front of Eltham Palace, engraved by Peter Stent, c.1653. The queen's apartments are to the left and the king's to the right
Below: An engraving of Eltham Palace from the north-east by Samuel and Nathaniel Buck, 1735. On the far left is a turret dating from 1316; its roof has now gone but the base survives

THE NORTH-EAST VIEW OF ELTHAM-PALACE, IN THE COUNTY OF KENT.

and Forests advocated demolition. A preservation campaign was mounted, led by the marquis of Lansdowne in the House of Lords. The campaign was successful and in 1828 the great hall was propped and repaired by Robert Smirke, an architect attached to the Office of Works.

Gentlemen's residences replaced the farm in the 19th century. The great hall became an indoor tennis court and flower and kitchen gardens were laid out in the west and south parts of the moat. Between 1894 and 1895 the Office of Works carried out minor repairs to the south bay of the great hall, funded by the Society for the Protection of Ancient Buildings. More substantially, in 1903 the 'temporary' props inserted by Smirke were removed and the roof trussed up with steel beams bolted on to the timber. The most extensive intervention occurred between 1911 and 1914, when Charles Peers, inspector of ancient monuments, and Frank Baines, architect in the Office of Works, dismantled the great hall roof and reassembled it, inserting steel braces to strengthen the weakened timbers. The hall was re-roofed with tiles, and much of the tracery renewed in the bay windows, but the hall was not fully restored until the Courtaulds acquired the site in the 1930s.

THE COURTAULDS

In 1933 Stephen and Virginia Courtauld sought a semi-rural property within easy reach of central London. Eltham met their requirements and they took a 99-year lease from the Crown. They commissioned the architects Seely and Paget to design a modern home on the site of the 19th-century buildings, while retaining as much as possible of the palace remains. They proposed a restrained exterior, faced with brick and Clipsham stone, inspired by Wren's Hampton Court Palace, on the mistaken assumption that Wren had 'restored', rather than sought to rebuild, the Tudor palace. They planned to conceal modern materials such as reinforced concrete.

Controversy

By 1933 the palace was almost surrounded by suburban development and Stephen Courtauld's proposal was welcomed as a means of halting the encroaching housing. There was nevertheless much debate about the propriety of building on to an ancient monument. Seely and Paget discussed their proposals with Sir Charles Peers, by now president of the Society of Antiquaries and chief inspector of ancient monuments with the Office of Works. Peers agreed with the general principle on

Left: A W Aumonier & Sons'
model of Eltham Palace
before works began in 1933.
Aumonier also made a
companion model showing
Seely and Paget's proposals
Below: The 15th-century
gables being propped in
1934. The intention was to
preserve them in situ, *but this
proved impossible and they
were subsequently dismantled,
restored and re-erected*

site in August 1933, but he had not seen any plans.
When these were later put before the Ancient
Monuments Board, Sir Patrick Duff, the permanent
secretary, was horrified. To pacify Duff, it was
agreed by the commissioners for Crown lands that
Seely and Paget would employ Peers (by this time
retired) as consultant architect for the restoration
of the great hall and north bridge. The Courtaulds
were also told that they had to preserve the
remains of the three 15th-century timber gables
east of the great hall.

In 1936 an article in *Architect and Building News*
was headed 'Romance dies at Eltham'. The
historian G M Young wrote in *The Times*: 'In order
to provide the tenant with a modern mansion,
three distinguished architects united their talents
and intelligence to destroy one of the most
beautiful things remaining in the neighbourhood of
London …The other day I found myself
confronted with what at first I took to be an
admirably designed but unfortunately sited
cigarette factory.' The architect Herbert Baker was
also critical. Gilbert Ledward countered, pointing
out that at Soane's Bank of England building Baker
had destroyed 'really beautiful work, while at
Eltham everything of historic interest and beauty
had been saved'.

Right: Stephen and Ginie
on board the Virginia,
in about 1935
Below: Gilbert Ledward's
carving on the loggia at
Eltham, showing Stephen's
sailing interests
Below right: Mah-Jongg in
his own deckchair on board
the Virginia

The Courtaulds' Travels

The Courtaulds'
yacht could
accommodate a
crew of almost 30
plus the Courtaulds
and six guests

The Courtaulds loved cruising in their yachts. In the mid-1920s they travelled abroad in their steam yacht *Eun Mara*. Stephen's brother-in-law Captain Wilfred Dowman (1880–1936), who had rescued and restored the *Cutty Sark*, helped Stephen design a new motor yacht *Virginia* in conjunction with G L Watson & Co. of Glasgow. The vessel combined the graceful design of steam yachts with the power of a motor yacht, having twin screw diesel engines. It was built by William Beardmore & Co. in Dalmuir in 1930. Measuring 210ft (64m) long with a 29ft 6in (9m) beam, and weighing over 700 tonnes, she had a long overhanging stern embellished with carved trailboards, and a clipper bow with a seahorse figurehead by the sculptor Harold Wilson Parker, who later designed the wren motif on the 1937 bronze farthing. Malacrida was responsible for designing the interior, which could accommodate a crew of almost 30 plus the Courtaulds and six guests.

The Courtaulds enjoyed spending long periods touring abroad. Their first Christmas after moving into Eltham was spent in Cairo as part of an African

tour from December 1936 to April 1937, including ten weeks flying from Egypt to South Africa and returning in the *Virginia* from Cape Town. Between 1937 and 1938 they flew to Ceylon (now Sri Lanka) where the *Virginia* was waiting for them to cruise around the South China Sea. Here they collected orchids and stored them on deck for propagation at Eltham. Ginie kept detailed typescript diaries of each journey and Stephen made cine films. On their return Ginie showed the films of their travels to the Royal Geographical Society in London.

1930S 'MOD-CONS'

Many of Eltham's technical features are taken for granted today, but in the 1930s they were at the cutting-edge of technology. By the mid-1930s Britain had one of the most advanced systems of electricity supply in the world. The Courtaulds took full advantage of this to enhance their new home. There were electric fires and synchronous clocks in most rooms, and a loudspeaker system that could broadcast records to rooms on the ground floor. Siemens installed a private internal telephone exchange. There was a centralized vacuum cleaner in the basement and the kitchen contained two Jackson's cookers and an electric Kelvinator refrigerator – appliances which were relatively rare at the time.

Gas was used to heat the hot water central heating which fed pipes embedded in the ceilings. In the entrance hall, great hall and bathrooms, however, the heating was beneath the floor, giving greater flexibility in room layouts.

Eltham's high standard of design and services can be compared with the Cunard Line's *Queen Mary* – the largest and most magnificent British liner ever built – which made her maiden voyage in May 1936. Elements of the *Queen Mary*'s luxurious Art Deco interiors echo those at Eltham, such as the wood panelling, plaster reliefs, abstract carpets by Marion Dorn and applied art. Just as at Eltham, a loudspeaker system broadcast music in selected areas on board and cabin-class suites had panelled interiors, electric clocks, built-in furniture and telephones linked by an internal exchange.

STEPHEN COURTAULD'S ART AND SCULPTURE COLLECTION

Stephen intended the new house to provide a setting for his art collection. He particularly favoured classically trained artists and sculptors who had studied at the British School in Rome, whose honorary general secretary, Sir Evelyn Shaw, was a close friend. In 1919 Stephen endowed a scholarship in engraving there and he served on its council from 1921 to 1947. Favoured Rome scholars included the painters Winifred Knights and Tom Monnington and the sculptors Gilbert Ledward, Charles Sargeant Jagger and Alfred Hardiman. Other contemporary artists included Muirhead Bone, Algernon Newton and Keith Baynes, who stayed regularly at Eltham.

Left: The basement motor of the centralized vacuum cleaner supplied by the British Vacuum Cleaner Company, London
Below: Andrea Mantegna's Descent into Limbo, painted in about 1492, was the star of Stephen's collection. It was bought in 1930 and once hung in the drawing room. It is now in a private collection

Following his experiences in the First World War he bought a number of war-related works at an Imperial War Museum exhibition in 1919, including pieces by Frank Brangwyn, C R W Nevinson and Charles Pears. Paul Nash's bleak watercolour *Hill 60* was purchased from the artist in 1920.

The collection also included earlier topographical artists such as J M W Turner, John Crome and Peter de Wint. The drawing room provided the setting for Stephen's collection of Italian Old Masters: two Veroneses, a Tintoretto, a Bellini, and the most significant painting of all – *Descent into Limbo* by Mantegna. All of them were purchased between 1927 and 1930, mostly from Agnews, the celebrated London dealers.

Above: The menu card for the duchess of York's visit in 1936 reveals that the champagne was 1923 Veuve Clicquot
Right: Stephen Gazelee (middle), in characteristic spats, red socks and Old Etonian bow tie, with Stephen Courtauld (standing) outside the dining room in 1940. Gazelee, 'the most erudite man in the world', and librarian at the Foreign Office, composed the Latin inscription in the great hall
Below: Portrait of Queen Elizabeth the Queen Mother (1900–2002) by John St Helier Lander, from The Illustrated London News, 15 May 1937. She visited Eltham in 1936 while still duchess of York

LIFE AT ELTHAM

The Courtaulds moved in on 25 March 1936. They established a daily routine comprising breakfast at 9am, lunch at 1pm, tea at 4.30pm and dinner at 8pm. Dinners at Eltham were not always a success, as Stephen and Ginie indiscriminately mixed people who had little in common. Furthermore, if Stephen was in one of his introspective moods, it was not unknown for him to sit through an entire meal without saying a word.

Eltham was self-consciously luxurious. In winter the rooms were if anything regarded as too hot, as the heating could not be zoned. All the baths could be run at the same time if necessary so that guests could dress for dinner in comfort. Cecil Beaton neatly captured the indolence of an English house party in an essay in *Vogue* in 1933: 'The clock strikes, and there is a cocktail to impregnate one with energy enough to move from the depth of the sofa, to climb the stairs, and then there is the extravagance of soaking in a bath cloudy with salts.'

Both Stephen and Ginie were keen on sport. Ginie was an ardent squash-player and in summer the Courtaulds and their guests used the swimming pool and tennis courts.

The grounds were opened to the public once a year. In the summer Ginie hosted 'at homes' commencing at 10pm and featuring fireworks and dancing well into the night. Annual summer fêtes and garden parties were also held. The Courtaulds also hosted large dinners: for Peter Peirano's 21st birthday celebration in July 1937 the royal confectioners Gunter & Co. supplied supper for 450 guests at ten shillings per head excluding drink, with entertainment provided by Lew Stone's celebrated dance band.

WARTIME ELTHAM

The routine of daily life at Eltham was irreversibly altered by the war. An inventory was made of the contents of the house in December 1939, and the principal paintings, antique carpets and tapestries were dispersed for safe-keeping. Most domestic staff left, and by the end of the war the original complement of about 15 gardeners had been reduced to two.

The Courtaulds lived at Eltham for much of the war, retreating to the basement during air raids. Both Stephen and Ginie contributed locally to the

Royal Visitors

Queen Mary had tea at Eltham on 4 July 1935 when she placed a silver jubilee medallion set in the tessellated floor of the loggia. She returned on 8 June 1938, by which time the gardens were more established. She commented: 'Eltham … has been done up by the Stephen Courtaulds who received me. The house is quite a modern one built by them, but the old Hall dating from the 14th century [sic] has been restored beautifully. We went all over the house and the charming moat garden and had tea in the Hall. A charming visit.'

Queen Elizabeth, the Queen Mother, regularly exchanged Christmas cards with the Courtaulds. She paid a private visit when still duchess of York on 12 July 1936: 'I like the Courtaulds very much, and loved their enthusiasm. I must say, that I thought some of the modern part a little overdone – but it was all very interesting, and my goodness what a good feed we had! And good champagne!'

war effort, Ginie as a local centre organizer for the Women's Voluntary Service and Stephen with the Civil Defence. At least eight of Stephen's close friends and relatives were involved with the Special Operations Executive (SOE), including the explorer George Binney, and August Courtauld, who laid explosives to scuttle French warships to prevent their use by Germany. George Courtauld was a personnel officer at the SOE and he took at least one new recruit to Eltham to brief him about the organization. The Courtauld firm helped finance the SOE, and Stephen may well have been involved himself.

In September 1940, during the battle of Britain, over 100 incendiary bombs fell on the estate, four of them striking the great hall and severely damaging the east end of the roof, because water from the Auxiliary Fire Service hoses could not reach over the windows. The damaged roof was protected by a temporary covering but in April 1941 this was blown off when a parachute mine exploded to the south of the estate.

Nevertheless, Courtauld hospitality continued. A friend later wrote: 'Even during the war, with no staff and no heating, everyone was sure of a warm welcome, with or without previous notice of their arrival or ration cards.'

In May 1944 the Courtaulds moved out of Eltham. London society had changed irrevocably, and the lack of servants meant it was impractical to continue living in a large house. The bombing had upset Ginie, and she also had to endure the death on active service of her nephew Paul.

Following several months of discussion it was agreed in March 1945 to give the remaining 88 years of the lease to the Army School of Education. Stephen's antique furniture was to remain in the great hall, and he was to be consulted over any future proposals to build in the grounds.

Left: The Arctic explorer Gino Watkins flanked by Paul and Peter Peirano, taken shortly before Watkins' fatal second expedition to Greenland in 1932. Stephen Courtauld had sponsored Watkins' first British Arctic Air Route Expedition of 1930–31
Below: *Courtauld family group on the lawn, photographed in 1941. Left to right: Stephen, Mollie, George, August and Ginie*

Right: Stephen in his mountaineering boots sketching at Loch Etive, Scotland, in about 1946

Below: One of Stephen's boots and mountaineering equipment carved by Gilbert Ledward on the loggia at Eltham

Below right: The Courtaulds' 1950s home, La Rochelle, Penhalonga, near Mutare, Zimbabwe, where Stephen and Ginie created an extensive botanic garden and arboretum

THE COURTAULDS AFTER ELTHAM

In September 1944 Stephen and Ginie settled in Scotland on the 24,000-acre Muckairn estate on the shore of Loch Etive, Argyll, where Stephen bred pedigree Highland cattle. The couple moved to Southern Rhodesia (now Zimbabwe) in 1951 and bought land near Umtali (now Mutare). They built a new house, called La Rochelle, after the home of Stephen's Huguenot ancestors in western France. Some of the architectural details were copied from Eltham, and they also installed the window from Eltham, where members of the royal family had written their signatures with a diamond.

In spite of increasing ill-health, Stephen participated vigorously in Rhodesian projects concerning social welfare and cultural life. He built two concert halls, a theatre, a multiracial residential club and a farming college. He helped fund University College, Salisbury, and was instrumental in establishing the Rhodes National Gallery in Salisbury to which he loaned and eventually bequeathed many of his works of art. He also wrote three volumes of *The Huguenot Family of Courtauld* (1957–67). He was knighted in 1958.

Stephen died in 1967 but Ginie remained at La Rochelle until 1970 when the war in Rhodesia prompted her to move to Jersey, where she remained until her death in 1972.

Weekends at Eltham

Mollie Butler (1907–2009), at the time married to Stephen's cousin August Courtauld, described a typical weekend at Eltham in the late 1930s:

'We'd arrive about teatime on the Friday, and have an enormous tea, with muffins and crumpets and everything. And Ginie always had a tiny little bottle of brandy on the tea table, which she put in people's tea. And then you'd go to your room, which was fearfully luxurious, with this bathroom with under-warming so you walked with bare feet on this warm marble floor. And enormous, wonderful towels which enveloped you. And wonderful bath oils, everything of the most luxurious.

'Dinner would be quite late. They'd have people in from London. Stephen was very keen on his film company so Michael Balcon [director of Ealing Studios] would be there and his daughter Jill Balcon. It was the sort of house where people would bring their friends, so Malcolm Sargent, the conductor would probably bring in some young person he wanted to push on in the world, and Ginie and Stephen would help. They were awfully good like that. They loved meeting potential artists, to whom they could offer hospitality and a push. During meals Ginie had a little pad and a silver pencil beside her, and anything she didn't like during the meal

she would write down to tell the chef. Everything had to be perfect.

'During the day, sometimes we gardened, Ginie was very keen on the garden and I used to help her. And there was a swimming pool and a squash court. Then on Sunday evening, more exhausted than alive really, because it had been quite hard work keeping up with Stephen and Ginie, we'd drive back to our home in London.'

Above: Replacement oak being carved for the great hall roof by the Ministry of Works in 1952

Right: An Army officers' conference at Eltham in the late 1960s

THE ARMY AT ELTHAM

From 1945 to 1992 Eltham was home to a number of different Army education units. Between 1945 and 1948 it was occupied by the officers' training wing of the Army School of Education, which produced *The General Education Handbook* – a full guide for army instructors.

In 1945 Eltham also became the home of the Army (later Royal Army) Educational Corps. Among the distinguished corps officers was Col Archie C T White, who served with the corps from 1920 until his retirement in 1947.

The Institute of Army Education (IAE) – an executive and research establishment of the Directorate of Army Education under the War Office – came to Eltham in 1948, administering educational examinations for the Army, teacher recruitment for Army children's schools overseas and further education for regular soldiers and officers. In 1983 another education unit, HQ Director of Army Education, replaced the IAE. This and the Royal Army Educational Corps remained at Eltham until 1992.

The Army's stewardship ensured the survival of the Courtauld wing at a time when the 1930s was out of fashion. Particularly farsighted was the decision to give the Dorn entrance hall rug to the Victoria and Albert Museum in the 1960s. Casualties of the desire for improvement in the 1980s, however, were the loss of nearly all of the original metal windows and the drastic remodelling of the Courtaulds' kitchen.

THE MINISTRY OF WORKS

The Ministry of Works (later the Department of the Environment) maintained the great hall and the palace remains. The hall was repaired and opened to the public, with the emphasis on the medieval work at the expense of the 1930s intervention. Unfortunately this included the destruction of the gondola-style Courtauld lanterns. The floor was the subject of considerable debate between the ministry's inspector and the Army. The inspector wanted a stone floor but the Army required a sprung floor for dancing. Eventually a compromise was reached: a stone floor was laid, but the Army was permitted to install a timber floor on top (now removed).

English Heritage assumed responsibility for the great hall in 1984. Since 1995, it has been actively restoring the gardens and interiors to their appearance in the time of the Courtaulds.